REAL STORIES. REAL BREAKTHROUGHS. REAL CHANGE

WHEN SHE FINALLY *Let Go!*

DR. PAULETTE HARPER

THY WORD PUBLISHING

Published by Thy Word Publishing
Antioch, CA 94531

© 2025 Dr. Paulette Harper

Book Cover Design: Tyora Moody
Interior Book Design & Formatting: https://tywebbincreations.com
Editor: Emile Kline http://ekediting.com/

Executive Book Mentor: Dr. Paulette Harper
Visit https://pauletteharper.com/pentopublish/ to access information about writing your own book.

All rights reserved. No part of this book may be used or reproduced, stored in or introduced into a retrieval system, or transmitted in any form including, photocopying, electronic or mechanical, recording or by any means without the express written consent from the author.

Scripture quotations marked "NKJV" are taken from the New King James Version. Copyright © 1982 by Thomas Nelson, Inc. Used by permission. All rights reserved.

Scripture quotations marked "KJV" are taken from the Holy Bible, King James Version, Cambridge, 1769. Used by permission.

Scriptures marked NIV are taken from the NEW INTERNATIONAL VERSION (NIV): Scripture taken from THE HOLY BIBLE, NEW INTERNATIONAL VERSION ®. Copyright© 1973, 1978, 1984, 2011 by Biblica, Inc.TM. Used by permission of Zondervan

Library of Congress Cataloging-in-Publication Data

Paperback: ISBN: 979-8-218-85580-2

Published and printed in the United States of America.

WHEN SHE FINALLY LET GO

Disclaimer

The views, opinions, and experiences shared in this book are those of the individual authors and do not necessarily reflect the views of the publisher. Each author is solely responsible for the content of their chapter, including any names, events, or personal stories mentioned.

The publisher assumes no responsibility for any claims, disputes, or legal matters arising from the inclusion of names or personal references in this book. By participating in this anthology, each author confirms that they have the right to use any names or references included in their chapter and have obtained necessary permissions where applicable.

If any individual referenced in this book has concerns regarding their inclusion, they should contact the respective author directly.

Contents

A Message from the Visionary Dr. Paulette Harper	VII
Acknowledgments	IX
Dedication	XI
Sponsors	XIII
Sponsors page 2	XIV
Introduction	XV
When the Weight Finally Lifted Dr. Paulette Harper	1
Running on Empty Dr. JoAnne Hayes	15
Wounds to Wisdom Carole M. Williams-Hayes	27
Tragedy Behind the Wrought Iron Gates Laura Costantino	41

The Words Within Her Lisa Council	55
Bag Lady Dr. LeAnn Cerise Hendrick	69
Shattered Pieces Lisa Richmond	81
Calling All Readers!	92
Write a Book With Me	94
Author Coaching Services Offered by Dr. Paulette Harper	96
Other Books By Dr. Paulette Harper	99

A Message from the Visionary

Dr. Paulette Harper

Twenty-Three-Times Best-Selling Author | Speaker | Pastor | Executive Book Mentor

When She Finally Let Go is more than an anthology—it's a divine movement of women who chose freedom over fear and purpose over pain. Within these pages, you'll encounter the stories of courageous women who made the life-altering decision to release what once held them captive—pain, shame, grief, toxic relationships, or self-doubt—and step fully into the destiny God designed for them.

Each story carries weight. These are not surface-level testimonies but deep, soul-stirring accounts of transformation. They are stories of women who broke generational cycles, reclaimed their voices, and found healing in surrender. Every chapter is a powerful reminder that what once crushed you can become the very message that sets someone else free.

It is my honor to share these stories with you, believing they will awaken something within you—faith to trust again, courage to release the past, and strength to walk boldly into your next season.

If you've ever wondered how to move forward after the breaking, may this book show you the beauty, grace, and power that come when you finally let go.

— *Dr. Paulette Harper*
Publisher & Visionary, *When She Finally Let Go*

Visit https://pauletteharper.com/signaturestoryworkbook/ to access a free recourse for aspiring authors.

Acknowledgments

To God be the glory—my source of wisdom, strength, and divine inspiration. Without His grace, this project would not exist. Every story, every breakthrough, and every moment of healing within these pages is a reflection of His redemptive power.

To the incredible women who said "yes" to sharing their stories—thank you. Your transparency, courage, and obedience have made this book what it is. You opened your hearts so others could find freedom, and through your words, lives will be changed.

To my editing and publishing team, your excellence and dedication helped bring this vision to life with beauty and precision. Thank you for believing in the mission and stewarding this project with care.

To my readers, I am deeply grateful. Your willingness to embrace these stories, reflect, and grow makes the journey worthwhile. My prayer is that this book strengthens your faith and reminds you that letting go is not the end—it's the divine beginning of something greater.

With love and gratitude,
— *Dr. Paulette Harper*
Publisher & Visionary, *When She Finally Let Go*

Dedication

To every woman who has ever carried the weight of her past,
to the one who prayed through the pain,
to the one who dared to release what no longer served her,
and to the one still learning to surrender—

This book is for you.

May these stories remind you that your healing is holy,
your journey is sacred,
and your breakthrough is closer than you think.
When you finally let go, you make room for God to move.

With love,

— *Dr. Paulette Harper*
Publisher & Visionary, *When She Finally Let Go*

"God is within her, she will not fall;
God will help her at break of day."
— **Psalm 46:5 (NIV)**

A Heartfelt Thank You to Our Sponsors

Thank you for believing in this vision before the world ever held it in their hands. Your support helped bring *When She Finally Let Go* from idea to impact, from manuscript to movement.

Your generosity, your investment, and your faith in this project have become part of its foundation. You didn't just purchase a book—you helped birth a message that will transform lives for years to come.

We honor you. We appreciate you.
And we are grateful that you chose to help us make history.
Thank you for being a Legacy Supporter of *When She Finally Let Go*.

Angela S Langhorne	Edward & Carmelita Williams III
Alicia Parks-Baxter	Elaine Wilson
Andrea L Mims	Erica R. Edge
Alicia Butler	Eulanda Cameron-Bethea
Angela P. Holman	Genise Capers
Amy Pebler	Gladys Espinoza
Anna Archila	Gloria Essian
Beverly Fleet	Gia Brantley
Bettina J. Sellers	Holleigh Norwood
Betty J. Hunter	Hurriel C. Harris CMSgt, USAF, Ret
Cherise Scott	Jennifer Abastillas
Clarence R. Crane, CMSgt, USAF, Ret	Jayla Brantley
Curtis & Tamica Reese	James Fleet
DeMetria White	Jacqueline Collier
David Smith	Jacquiline Cox
Darryl Harris	Jada M. Hayes
Dorothy M Steele	Jasmine M. Williams-Hayes, SSgt, USAF
Dr. Sheila D. Williams	Johnie & Jada Stevens
Duncan E. Siler	Julius Rhodes
Evelyn Nijem	James Hayes
Ella Brantley	Joannie Hayes
Earline Dowdell	

A Heartfelt Thank You to Our Sponsors

Juvante' M. Hayes
Juwan M. Hayes
Karen Gordon
Kevin Linder
Kevin Scruggs
Kathy McKnight
Kristen Simpson
Kyi Branch
Kim Tolero
Lulu Nino-Flores
LaKisha Copeland
Lewis Nelson
Lillie White
Maria Gonzalez
Marilyn Holland
Maria Long
Marcia Higgins
M. White
Martha Brown
Nichole Wynn

Patricia Jackson
Patricia Fowler
Robin Branch
Robin Middleton
Rosetta Copeland
Sandra Hallums
Simone Richmond
Susan Richmond
Sharon Washington
Shirley Green
Terry West
Tonya Crawley
T'Maya Simmons
Taft and Angie Mitchell Jr
Tammy Harper
Travis L. Millner
Tracy Washington
Wilynda Fuller

Introduction

There comes a moment in every woman's life when holding on becomes heavier than letting go.

For years, many of us have carried silent weights—pain from the past, shame from decisions we wish we could undo, fear of stepping into the unknown. We've held on to broken relationships, unfulfilled dreams, and the need to appear strong while quietly crumbling inside. But there is freedom on the other side of release.

When She Finally Let Go is more than an anthology—it's a movement of women who chose healing over hiding, surrender over striving, and faith over fear. Each chapter carries the heartbeat of a woman who made the courageous decision to release what once defined her, and in doing so, discovered the God who restores, renews, and redeems.

These stories are raw, real, and redemptive. They remind us that letting go isn't a sign of weakness—it's a sacred act of trust. When we release what was never meant to be ours to carry, we make room for God to do what only He can do: transform our pain into purpose and our wounds into wisdom.

As you turn each page, my prayer is that you will find your own moment of release—that you'll see yourself reflected in these pages and know that it's your time to let go.

— *Dr. Paulette Harper*
Publisher & Visionary, *When She Finally Let Go*

WHEN THE WEIGHT FINALLY LIFTED

Dr. Paulette Harper

For twenty-three years, I built my life around a marriage I believed would last forever. I wore the titles of wife, co-pastor, and mother with pride. My world revolved around creating stability for my family, serving in ministry, and fulfilling what I thought was my God-given role as a wife. I imagined we would grow old together, celebrate grandchildren, and someday, look back over decades of shared memories with a smile. But that dream unraveled piece by piece, until one day, it was gone altogether.

I walked into our bedroom and noticed the growing pile of household items in the corner. Pots and pans stacked neatly beside folded towels, boxes filled with random necessities—all the things one would gather when preparing to move. It was a silent but undeniable signal of an impending departure. Eventually, the pile vanished, but so did he. The space sat empty, his belongings gone, his presence erased as if he had never lived there at all.

The weight of abandonment crashed into me. I dropped to my knees, curled in on myself, and sobbed until I could barely breathe. My tears soaked the carpet as I cried out to God for answers, for relief, for anything that would ease the pain of rejection. Twenty-three years of marriage ended in silence, leaving me with nothing but questions, confusion, and a broken heart.

Sis, have you ever experienced a moment when the life you built disappeared overnight? Have you ever stood in the middle of your own home and felt like a stranger in the ruins of what used to be? That's what I carried. That's what I had to let go of.

I wanted to cling to the life I had known. I wanted to hold on to the picture-perfect family, the ministry, and the security of being someone's wife. But I realized I had to let go of the marriage, the identity I had tied to being a wife, and the illusion that my worth depended on someone else's decision to stay. I had to release the bitterness and shame that threatened to bury me. Most of all, I had to let go of the belief that my future was over just because one chapter of my life had ended.

The surrender process was not clean or easy. It was messy, raw, and painful. There were nights when my silent home felt deafening, when I cried until my body ached. In those early days, I wrestled with feelings of rejection so deep they nearly convinced me I was unworthy of love. In my darkest hours, overwhelmed by the ache of loss and the fear of a future I didn't recognize, I even thought about ending my life. That thought shocked me, frightened me, and pushed me to reach for help before I sank any further.

I prayed, sometimes through clenched teeth, other times through sobs I could barely form into words. I opened my Bible looking for comfort and stumbled across verses that became lifelines. One in particular spoke directly to my heart: "So David inquired of the LORD, saying, 'Shall I pursue this troop? Shall I overtake them?' And He answered him, 'Pursue, for you shall surely overtake *them* and without fail recover *all*'" (1 Samuel 30:8 NKJV). Those words reminded me that even though I had lost something precious, God had not abandoned me. He promised recovery.

But surrender still required me to face resistance within myself. I resisted starting over. I resisted the reality of being single after decades of marriage. I resisted the unfamiliar road God was asking me to walk. Yet slowly, through prayer, journaling, quiet moments of reflection, and therapy, I began to release my grip on the past. I reached out—to a counselor, to trusted friends, to scripture—and the lone thread of connection I found pulled me back from the edge. Surrender came in waves. It was not a single moment of handing everything over to God, but a daily choice to trust Him with the broken pieces of my life.

Sis, what would it look like for you to unclench your hands from what is hurting you? What would shift if you chose, day by day, to trust God with the pieces you cannot put back together? Who can you call today to keep you from carrying the weight alone?

In that season of pain, God gave me an unexpected assignment: write a book. What I was going through was not in vain. Writing became another form of therapy—a place to lay the grief down and name it, to trace the edges of my hurt until it made sense. Each word was a step toward healing. Each chapter was an act of surrender. By the time my book, *That Was Then, This Is Now: This Broken Vessel Restored*, was finished, I realized that God had not only healed me but also given me a new purpose.

Letting go changed everything. It opened the door to a future I could never have imagined while I was still holding on to the pain. I discovered gifts and talents I didn't know existed. I discovered resilience I didn't know I had. God birthed in me a new vision for my life, one that extended beyond the walls of the church into the broader world.

While married, I had been content with serving as co-pastor, caring for my children, and working a 9-to-5 job. That was the life I knew, and I was comfortable with it. But when everything changed, God pushed me out of my comfort zone. The unfamiliar road I traveled became the very path He had designed for me all along. Writing that first book set me on a journey that has now spanned decades—coaching authors, leading collaborations, building businesses, hosting events, and speaking on stages I never thought I would stand on.

Sis, what could be waiting on the other side of your surrender? What untapped gifts are hidden inside of you, waiting for pressure and pain to bring them to the surface? Who might you become if you allowed God to work through the broken places?

I discovered that pain can be the birthplace of purpose. The rejection I endured became the foundation for resilience. And the shame I carried was replaced with confidence rooted in God's plan for my life.

When I finally let go, miracles unfolded. Book after book was created, each one carrying a piece of my testimony. Doors opened to collaborations with authors who needed guidance to tell their own stories. A coaching business was born, giving me the privilege of walking alongside hundreds of authors as they wrote, published, and shared their books with the world. My influence expanded beyond what I thought possible—through my book tours, my publishing services, and the ministries that grew out of one simple yes to God.

Letting go taught me that even when everything falls apart, God's hand is still on His children. He used the season of loss to show me strength I didn't know I had. He gave me fresh vision, new dreams, and a broader assignment. I learned that my worth was never in who stayed or who left—it was in who God created me to be.

Looking back, I can clearly see that what I once viewed as my breaking point was actually the birthing point of a new season. The weight that once felt unbearable became the very pressure that pushed me into purpose. What the enemy meant for my destruction, God used as the catalyst for transformation. He didn't just mend my broken heart—He rebuilt me from the inside out.

For years, my identity was intertwined with being a wife, a co-pastor, and the keeper of a life I thought would last forever. But in letting go, I discovered who I truly was apart from titles, roles, and expectations. I met *me*—the woman God had been shaping all along. I found strength in my vulnerability, courage in my surrender, and clarity in my silence with God. Each "yes" to Him became a brick in the new foundation He was laying for my life.

Sis, I don't know what weight you're carrying today. Maybe it's the grief of an ended relationship, the pain of a deferred dream, or the fear of starting over. I do know this: God meets us in the breaking. He specializes in taking shattered pieces and creating something breathtakingly new. You don't need all the answers; you just have to release your grip and trust Him with the outcome.

Letting go is not weakness—it is spiritual strength. It's the moment heaven leans in to partner with your surrender. It's where the ashes of yesterday give way to the beauty of tomorrow.

As I reflect on that season now, I realize that the true miracle wasn't simply surviving—it was *becoming*. The woman who once wept on the floor, broken and unsure, is not the same woman standing today. God didn't just restore what I lost; He redefined who I was becoming. He exchanged my ashes for beauty, my despair for joy, and my fear for a fierce, unshakable faith.

Every tear watered the soil of a new vision. Every step forward, no matter how trembling, became evidence of His sustaining grace. And with each act of surrender, I began to see that the end of one chapter was simply God turning the page to something far greater.

The Word reminds us in Isaiah 43:18–19 (NIV): *"Forget the former things; do not dwell on the past. See, I am doing a new thing! Now it springs up; do you not perceive it? I am making a way in the wilderness and streams in the wasteland."*

Sis, the same is possible for you. There's a version of you on the other side of letting go—stronger, wiser, more radiant, and fully aligned with God's purpose. But she only emerges when you release what's weighing you down. Trust that God knows what He's doing. Trust that He can carry what you cannot.

This is your invitation to rise. Not in your own strength, but in the strength of the One who never left you. Lay it down. Release the weight. Step into the new chapter God has already written.

Because letting go is not the end of your story—it's the moment heaven rewrites your future with grace and power.

And when you finally let the weight lift, you won't just *survive* the loss... you'll *soar* into purpose.

DR. PAULETTE HARPER

About the Author

Dr. Paulette Harper is an ordained pastor, a twenty-tree time best-selling and two-time award-winning author. She is the visionary founder of Build-Her Kingdom Women, a faith-based movement equipping Christian women to lead with purpose, power, and biblical integrity in both ministry and the marketplace. Through mentorship, teaching, and live events, she empowers women to rise as builders of legacy and impact.

She is also the founder of The Reset Encounter, a transformational experience designed to help women reset their lives spiritually, emotionally, and mentally. Through retreats, intimate gatherings, and sacred encounters with God, The Reset Encounter guides women into breakthrough, healing, and a renewed sense of identity and purpose.

In recognition of her leadership and lifelong service, Dr. Harper was honored with the 2024 Rise-Her Presidential Lifetime Achievement Award and the Passion Purpose Peace Award, presented by Her Excellency Dr. Theresa A. Moseley.

As the founder and CEO of Harper Media, she serves as an Executive Book Mentor to aspiring nonfiction authors—specializing in coaching women to build their brand, expand their influence, and publish impactful books that establish them as subject matter experts in their field.

Connect with Dr. Paulette Harper

Website: www.pauletteharper.com

Publisher's Reflection

When I look back on that season of my life, I see more than pain—I see the hand of God weaving purpose through every broken place. What felt like the end of everything familiar became the birthplace of a new assignment. In the quiet moments when the house echoed with loss, God was already writing the next chapter. What the enemy meant to break me became the very thing God used to build me.

Sis, maybe you're standing where I once stood—surrounded by the fragments of a life that no longer exists, holding memories in one hand and unanswered questions in the other. Let me remind you: surrender is not the end; it's the turning point. When I finally unclenched my hands and released what I couldn't control, God met me there. He didn't just mend the broken pieces—He reshaped my life, redefined my identity, and set me on a path I never saw coming.

Letting go was not a single act; it was a daily decision to trust Him with my future. It required courage to face the unknown and faith to believe that what lay ahead was greater than what I had lost. And He proved Himself faithful. He gave me beauty for ashes, opened doors I didn't know existed, and showed me a version of myself I had never met before.

If you're carrying a heavy weight, I want you to hear this: God specializes in rewriting stories. Your tears are not wasted. Your surrender is seen. And the chapter you thought was an ending might just be the beginning of something extraordinary.

Trust Him. Release it. Rise.

— *Dr. Paulette Harper*
Publisher & Visionary, *When She Finally Let Go*

Running on Empty

Dr. JoAnne Hayes

Between work, church, family, friends, and my personal life, I poured myself out until there was nothing left of me. Saying "yes" was no longer a choice—it was my identity. People saw me as dependable, the one they could always call, and I wore that like a badge of honor. But what started as service slowly turned into bondage. My willingness to please became a habit I couldn't shake, even when I was tired, even when I was hurting, even when no one said thank you anymore. The more I showed up, the less I felt seen. I was running on empty, trying to please everyone while silently breaking inside.

The Hayes Helper Handbook: Closed for Healing

It wasn't until I finally let go—of the guilt, of the constant striving, of the need to be everything to everyone—that I discovered the power of setting boundaries for me and my peace of mind. Letting go didn't mean I stopped loving people. It meant I started loving myself enough to stop living depleted.

I was addicted to a powerful tool called *acceptance*. My desire to fit in created the role of always being there for others. This was learned and self-taught behavior. As a child, I took care of others. It was not an option. At age twelve, I was caring for my siblings and helping them with their homework. With my mother's instruction, I made dinner and on Saturdays and did the laundry. I was in the role.

This led me to believe that I had to help anyone close to me; I had to take the lead as a helper. If someone asked, I could not refuse. Sometimes, I would offer before the question was asked. I became the *Hayes: I Will Do It Book for Helpers*. If I did not have the answer right away, I found the answer.

My needs and wants were put on the back burner, but I had no idea I was putting myself last. Why would I do this to myself? Because, at some point, I did not possess self-acceptance. I thought helping was what I was supposed to do, that it was the reason I was on this earth. My true identity slowly slipped away every time I assumed the role. I had no idea how exhausted I was at times.

The desire to be accepted took a toll on me and my body. I was always there for others, even when they were not there for me. Afterward, I would feel bad about putting myself out there. So, me, myself, and I had a great conversation, and we decided that "Next time, I will not volunteer to help. If asked, I will say no." But when acceptance reared its ugly head and I was asked to help, once again, no was not an option.

Finally Choosing Me: A Reflection on Saying No

As a beautiful, educated, and mature adult, I am finally seeing the light. In 2025, I realized that I could say no and be okay. The person asking would be okay, too.

I was unaware of the physical side effects, the emotional and mental anguish when I did not trust my gut instinct because I thought I was doing the right thing. Consciously, I did not realize I sought acceptance. But unconsciously, I was. I had internalized it. Growing up, I only saw my mom's strength. I thought that was how I was supposed to be. If there was pain, my motto was "Never let them see you sweat." So, I cried in silence.

Years of neglecting myself, of not protecting my mental health, of internalizing everything brought on sleepiness nights, weight gain, stress, and anxiety. Then one day, I broke down. I was surviving on the fumes of wanting to be accepted. *I was running on empty.*

So, I prayed and asked God to help me. I asked Him to please teach me how to say no. I begged Him to take away that desire to be in that role. I cried and prayed myself to sleep.

The buzzing of my cell phone woke me up. It was a text message from someone asking for a favor. I answered; I did not say no. Instead, I said, *I am just waking up. Give me some time to think about it. I will call you and let you know.* I guess I took too long. I got a *never mind* text, but it did not bother me.

Have you ever felt like you've taken one step forward and two steps back? Have you ever said "yes" so often that you forgot what it felt like to breathe, to rest, to simply be? After saying "yes," have you ever felt a tightness in your chest or your heart rate increasing? That is your body trying to protect you from *you*.

I had to learn that letting go didn't mean I stopped loving people—it meant I started loving myself enough to protect my peace. And you can, too. It's okay to say no. It's okay to rest. It's okay to choose you. Because when you finally let go, you discover the freedom God designed for your life. Positive thinking isn't just a mindset—it's the armor I wear daily, forged in faith.

Everyone's path is different. Maybe your path can look like this:

Give yourself permission to pause before answering.

Set one healthy boundary this week and honor it.

Trust that people will be okay even if you don't show up every time.

Learn to say "no" as an act of self-love, not rejection.

Believe that your worth is not tied to how much you do, but who you are in Christ.

For years, I believed my worth was tied to how much I could do for others. I wore "yes" like a medal, not realizing it was slowly weighing me down. But learning to let go—of guilt, unrealistic expectations, and the desperate need for acceptance—became my turning point. It wasn't easy. It required honest conversations with myself, tearful prayers, and uncomfortable moments of silence after a "no." But it was necessary.

Letting go didn't happen overnight. It was a daily choice to trust God's strength over my striving. Each "no" became a small act of courage, and each boundary became a brick in the foundation of my healing. I started to see that my value was never in the doing—it was in simply being who God created me to be.

Today, I walk in a new kind of strength—not the kind that demands perfection, but the kind that flows from grace. I no longer run on empty; I rise from a place of fullness, faith, and freedom. And so can you.

Here are a few affirmations:

I learn something new every day and grow stronger through it.

God is healing every broken place in me, even the ones I cannot see.

I am surrounded by grace, guided by faith, and held by divine love.

Every breath I take is a step toward wholeness.

No weapon formed against me shall prosper.

I am walking in my purpose, grace, and strength each day.

Sis, maybe you see yourself somewhere in my story. Maybe you've been carrying the weight of everyone else's needs while quietly neglecting your own. I want you to know this: you are allowed to choose *you*. You are allowed to protect your peace. You are allowed to rest. Saying "no" does not make you less loving; it makes you whole.

About the Author

As a co-author in *When She Finally Let Go*, Dr. JoAnne Hayes is a visionary leader with expertise in business administration, legal strategy, and servant leadership. Guided by her mantra—"Learn something new every day"—she promotes lifelong learning and educational equity. A passionate literacy advocate, she empowers others through mentorship and example.

Dr. Hayes is a best-selling co-author of *My Walk Past Hell, For Such a Time as This,* and *Virtuous & Victorious,* and has been featured in *Success Women's Magazine* and on *Called to Inspire, The Kim Jacobs Show, OWN IT,* and *WJNI 106.3 FM.* She earned her bachelor's degree from North Carolina A&T State University and her doctorate from Walden

University during the pandemic. A proud member of Zeta Phi Beta Sorority, Inc., she serves on the Survivor's Council and mentors' youth in her faith-based community.

Connect with Dr. JoAnne

https://linktr.ee/drjoannehayes

Publisher's Reflection

As I read Dr. JoAnne's story, I felt the weight of so many women's silent struggles—the constant "yes," the hidden tears, the quiet exhaustion that becomes a way of life. Her journey is one that echoes through generations of women who have been taught to hold everything together, even when they're breaking inside. She beautifully reveals what happens when we finally give ourselves permission to pause, to breathe, and to say "no" without guilt.

Sis, maybe you've found yourself in that same cycle—pouring until there's nothing left, believing that love means overextending, that service requires self-neglect. But Dr. JoAnne's chapter reminds us that letting go isn't abandonment; it's alignment. It's the holy decision to honor the vessel God created you to be. You were never designed to run on empty. God's desire is for you to live in a place of fullness, not constant depletion.

Choosing "no" can be one of the most spiritual decisions you make. Each boundary you set is not rebellion—it's protection. It's a declaration that you value the assignment God has placed in your life enough to guard your peace. This kind of letting go requires courage, honesty, and faith. But as Dr. JoAnne shows us, on the other side of that "no" is freedom—the kind that allows you to walk boldly in your purpose, unburdened and whole.

Take a moment and ask yourself: Where have you been saying "yes" out of obligation instead of obedience? What would happen if you trusted God enough to rest? Remember, your worth is not tied to how much you do. It's anchored in who you are—chosen, loved, and called.

— *Dr. Paulette Harper*
Publisher & Visionary, *When She Finally Let Go*

Wounds to Wisdom
Carole M. Williams-Hayes

Have you ever looked back and realized that a younger, wounded version of you has been making decisions all along? That was me. My wounded inner child led me to marry two emotionally absent men because I was raised by emotionally unavailable parents. I was searching for the love I didn't receive as a little girl. But healing doesn't start with getting married or happen through others—it starts by facing yourself.

You may recall a "happy" childhood, but others, like myself, remember feeling isolated and confused. Did my parents set out to be emotionally unavailable? No, not at all. They were trying to recover from things they had not addressed in their lives. My trauma was never intentional, and it's not about what happened, but what didn't—the lack of emotional responsiveness and validation from my parents.

As a young child—up to about age nine and prior to my dad *really* living for God—I looked to my parents as role models for engaging with others. I didn't know that the fights, the lying, and the drinking I observed were dysfunctional. While both my parents were detached, the dynamic with an emotionally unavailable mother can have unique impacts. Mothers are often the primary caregivers and are traditionally expected to nurture children. When this expectation is unmet, it can create a deep, traumatic sense of loss and confusion that remains until adulthood. Almost everyone is carrying some type of pain or trauma. It's how we respond to that pain that separates us.

My parents offered me sporadic love and support. Warm and affectionate one day, then distant and preoccupied the next, they created confusion and insecurity about when or if I would receive affection again. My dynamic with my mother had a greater impact on me because Dad was the breadwinner and gone for most of the day while Mom was a housewife. My mother set unrealistically high expectations, which led to a cycle of striving for perfection and inevitable failure. This constant criticism damaged my self-esteem and caused me to overthink everything, which carried over into my adult life. I felt so baffled that I cried to God, asking, "What is wrong with me?"

Things grew so dire that I once removed a razor from the bathroom cabinet to cut my wrists to end my pain. That is when I heard a voice say, "The Lord is close to the brokenhearted and saves those who are crushed in spirit" (Psalm 34:18 NIV).

Today, I am in my senior season of adulthood, and I work daily by praying, maintaining a support system of friends and family, and seeing a therapist to heal my wounded inner child. Are you wondering how that wounded child continues showing up despite the outward appearance of having it all together? The truth is, sometimes, I feel a persistent void or sense that something crucial is missing, stemming from my unmet emotional needs. Here are some of my behaviors that you might relate to if you've also grown up with emotionally unavailable parents:

The tendency to enter abusive or unstable relationships: I did not have a clear picture of what a healthy relationship looked like growing up. Because of this, I easily fell into patterns of dysfunctional relationships as both the abuser and the victim, depending on the circumstance.

People-pleasing: I adopted people-pleasing behaviors to get my needs met. However, that was only temporary and superficial most of the time. I would go to great lengths to fill that void of love, and if it wasn't for my Christian upbringing, by seeking this type of intimacy regularly, I learned through therapy that sex addictions can develop, and I wanted no part of that.

Self-esteem issues: not receiving enough affection or attention growing up affected my sense of self-worth, leaving me feeling unlovable.

The inability to state my emotional needs: As a child, my emotional needs were rejected for extended periods of time. Those feelings stayed with me into adulthood because I never felt safe. God has allowed me grace and time to learn as a parent of four that each child has certain needs and no two children are alike. Every day, I'm so amazed at how lucky I am to be a mom. Despite all my struggles and all the hardships I've faced while existing in survival mode, they are the one thing I got right. I invested 100% in them, and I have seen the return on my investment. One day, I told my youngest son, "I always wanted to make sure that I kept things equal among the four of you."

He replied, "No, Mom, it will never be equal because we all have different needs; however, you have always been fair." That's when I knew I had gotten it right and that I had broken a generational curse.

If you had emotionally unavailable parents growing up, you may feel unable to be emotionally present in relationships and struggle with empathy or discerning your own emotional needs. You may have a wounded inner child in you, so please reflect.

The above-mentioned behaviors are not all I have worked on to keep my wounded inner child from constantly showing up in my adult life. It took a lot of self-reflection, questioning, soul searching, and breakthrough moments before I was able to come to these realizations and start the process of letting go. I asked myself questions like "Why did I hold onto so many wrong people for so very long? Why was I so scared to walk away when I knew that the relationship was all wrong for me?" They say hindsight is 20/20, but so is wisdom. You get more of both when you grow older, become emotionally mature, and there's nothing like looking into a mirror to help you put your entire life into perspective. I found spiritual strength (faith) very early in life because I knew that I didn't want my pain to define my story or let it break me. Life is about choices, and I chose to channel my pain to push me to my purpose.

One day, while I was getting dressed for work in the military, I stopped to examine myself in the mirror and started to cry as the previous day's events played in my head. My primary doctor informed me after a physical that my psychological feelings and physical reactions—restlessness, feeling on edge, increased heart rate, shortness of breath, and difficulty concentrating—warranted a prescription for Zoloft to alleviate my anxiety. I asked, "Doc, are you saying that I'm crazy?" This was the beginning of learning how my wounded inner child had affected not only my physical health but my mental health as well.

Another day, when I was visiting my parents while on leave from the military, out of the blue and from her dementia/MS-ridden bed, my mother said to me, "I have always felt sorry for you."

I felt like she had kicked me between my legs and the pain ended in my throat and knocked the wind out of my body. That was the one time my dad stood up for me and said, "No, Mattie, that's not nice."

My mother's words took me back to the five-year-old who only ever wanted her unconditional love. I walked away that time, thinking, *No, Mom, I'm sorry that you were unable to really love me the way I loved you.*

Therapy Helped Me Divorce Toxic Ways

Many people, like myself, get divorced, but rarely do any of us divorce the version of ourselves or our marriage that didn't serve us. We walk away from our partner but never divorce the toxic, hurtful, unhealthy patterns that poisoned the relationship in the first place.

After many months of attending therapy with a Christian counselor, after sharing my behaviors arising from my wounded inner child, I said to my therapist, "I am sick of being the black sheep in my family."

She asked me, "Do you feel that it is a bad thing?"

"To be honest, no, because the 'black sheep' is usually the one breaking toxic cycles."

"Then how can that be bad?"

This was the start of a breakthrough and attracting fewer dysfunctional people as I let go of what didn't serve me. I can discern in my spirit when it is time to change, move on from people, or divorce unhealthy habits. Every time I level up by choosing me, I lose a bad habit, a toxic friendship, a dysfunctional relationship, and a useless version of myself. It's never a loss, but a gain. Sometimes, God closed doors because he knew I wasn't going to move unless circumstances forced me to and I trusted the transition.

No matter what life has thrown at each of us, there comes a time when we must let go of blaming, let go of how we were raised and the environment we came from. Blaming holds us back from the future. Growth is a decision, and what each of us wants for our lives is our choice. Remember, God gave us free will. Replace blaming with healing because it shows accountability for oneself. Healing is our responsibility alone. "Never regret a day in your life. Good days give happiness, bad days give experience, worst days give lessons, and best days give memories" (Anonymous).

Sometimes, we meet people such as family, friends, and therapists who leave a lasting impression on our souls. But the greatest person you will ever meet is yourself, like I did when I stopped accepting anything less than what I deserve. I have struggled, survived, rehabilitated, and recovered from relationships that should have had me committed and in a straitjacket. But one by one, stressful things are exiting my life and being replaced with blessings.

Having grace is a beautiful thing. My parents may have been emotionally unavailable, but they did their best with what they had, their knowledge, wounds, and capacity. It may not have been enough for what I needed, but they gave all they had. Forgiveness and understanding created peace in my heart.

DR. PAULETTE HARPER

I've spent so many years trying to survive and hold on, but sometimes, the most powerful transformation isn't about holding on, it's about... *When I Finally Let Go!*

About the Author

Carole M. Williams-Hayes served in the U.S. Air Force for twenty-four years and is a John Maxwell Speaker and Life Recovery Coach with a passion for empowering souls through servant leadership. She holds three master's degrees—in Management Leadership, Human Resources, and Social Work.

She shares her story as a co-author in ***When She Finally Let Go***. Carole is a nationally certified Sexual Assault, Domestic Violence, and Child Advocate, as well as a Mental Health and Substance Use Recovery Specialist, currently working as a Registered Clinical Intern Therapist. Her greatest joy is spending time with her young adult children—Jasmine, Jada, Juwan, and Juvanté—and her motto is, "I'd rather see a sermon than hear one any day!"

Connect with Carole

Email: cmwilliamshayes4@gmail.com

Instagram/Facebook: @caroleamethystrose9

Publisher's Reflection

In ***Wounds to Wisdom***, Carole opens the door to a truth many quietly carry—that healing often begins when we finally face the parts of ourselves we've long avoided. Her story is a tender yet powerful reminder that emotional wounds don't simply disappear with age; they follow us until we choose to confront them in God's light.

Through vulnerability and courage, Carole shows what it means to meet the wounded inner child and speak healing over her. She takes us from pain to purpose, from self-blame to breakthrough, and from survival to surrender. What once held her hostage—rejection, people-pleasing, and the echoes of childhood pain—became the very soil where wisdom and grace took root.

Carole's transparency is her ministry. Her words pierce deeply because they're written from a place of truth—a woman who has chosen to divorce her toxic patterns, not just her past relationships. That level of freedom only comes through God's guidance and the hard work of inner transformation.

Her story reminds us that growth requires accountability, healing demands honesty, and freedom begins with forgiveness—even toward those who couldn't love us the way we needed.

Carole teaches that *letting go isn't losing; it's making room for what God wants to plant next.* Every tear, every therapy session, every surrendered prayer became her stepping stone toward wholeness. And as she beautifully declares, "Sometimes, the most powerful transformation isn't about holding on—it's about letting go."

— *Dr. Paulette Harper*
Publisher & Visionary, ***When She Finally Let Go***

Tragedy Behind the Wrought Iron Gates

Laura Costantino

In 1985, in my Humanities class, they showed us pictures of the Carolands Mansion in Hillsborough, CA. This beautiful ninety-two-room château nestled in the hills was run down; no one had lived in it since the 1970s. There was talk of a security guard who would give girls unauthorized tours. Curious, my friends and I drove up there three or four times to see if the security guard would let us in. On our fourth try, he came out to the broken chain-link fence where we were parked and told us to come back on Friday for the tour.

On Friday, we walked up the long uphill driveway that led to the mansion. To get to the front door, we had to walk through a foyer, where we saw a car backed in. We didn't think anything of it. The security guard told us we had to be quiet and stay away from the windows because police patrolled the area with dogs, and he could get in trouble. He acted like a tour guide, telling us all kinds of information about the property. We started in the basement, creepy, dark, with minimal lights on the massive walls. Rooms stood on both sides, and one had a large table at least two feet thick. We walked in a single-file line, each of us holding the back of the person's shirt in front of us.

The house was magnificent. The history and architectural designs were breathtaking, even as rundown as it was. Outside one of the many kitchens, the security guard said, "There's a hidden floor. Do you want to see it?"

We declined, though I'm not sure why. As we reached the top floor, we came upon an exquisite room with an oval ceiling beautifully painted with a Michelangelo replica. It got weird when he told us, "I bring nude models here and photograph them. I'm a professional photographer."

We simply ignored him.

Next, we came to a room with double doors—a photography room. "Let's do this," he said. "One of you go into the room, and I'll lock it. I want you to scream as loud as you can."

One friend went in, and he shut the door. We couldn't hear her scream at all. We asked him to let her out. There was a long pause, maybe five minutes, where he just stared at us silently. We begged him to open the door. Finally, he unlocked it, and she came out. Thank you, Jesus! We were terrified, though we didn't say anything to each other. Something was very wrong.

"I told my friend where we are," I lied, hoping it would scare him from doing anything. No one knew where we were.

As we made our way down from the massive château, he asked if we wanted to visit the hidden floor again to see another kitchen. We declined.

We reached the beautiful double-sided staircase, and I asked if he could take a picture of us with my Kodak Instamatic camera. He held it backward and couldn't figure out how to use it—even though he'd just said he was a professional photographer. We exchanged a look that said everything, thanked him, and as soon as we reached the door, we ran down the hill toward the main road, crying.

Eight days later, on Sunday evening, I was watching the ten o'clock news when I heard the words, "Coming up next: murder at the château." A picture of a security guard appeared on the screen—it was him. He was accused of murdering a young girl.

Fear would consume me for the next thirty-four years.

I testified in two high-profile trials within three years. Nothing shook me more than when the judge said, "You and your two friends are lucky young ladies. Thankfully, your third friend came along. When there are three people, one can always run." The homicide sergeant later told us that he had planned it for my friend and me but changed his mind. That man now sits on death row in San Quentin.

The thought haunted me—*it could have been us.* I once read, "Faith and fear both ask you to believe in something you can't see. The one you choose writes your future" (Bob Proctor). I unintentionally chose fear. I was consumed by survivor's guilt. Someone died, and we were spared. It felt like a part of me was trapped between gratitude for being alive and deep sorrow that it came at such a high cost.

Fear gripped me so hard I could physically feel it, and it weighed me down daily. There are moments in life that change you—or scar you. Grow you or paralyze you. I was a senior in high school, innocent and trusting, and then overnight, I trusted no one and feared everyone. I was emotionally traumatized.

Have you ever faced a fear that deep?

I slowly evolved into what people call a "helicopter parent"—a parent who is overly involved in their children's lives, constantly hovering over them like a helicopter. I thought if I stayed close enough, I could protect them so nothing like what happened to me would ever happen to them.

It comforted me, knowing where they were and who they were with. I created a fun, safe place not only for my own children but for others, too. I always had a home-cooked meal ready because when my kids were home, I could finally breathe easier.

My need for control came from fear. Deep down, I was protecting myself from ever having to experience what that mother went through when she lost her only child. I couldn't bear the thought of something tragic happening to mine.

This wasn't healthy, but I didn't know what normal looked like. It felt like being caught in a web—every thought, emotion, and behavior pulling tighter the more I struggled. My emotions and actions were tangled together, and I thought being in control would make life easier. Instead, it turned into sleepless nights, obsessive cleaning, checking locks, and making sure everything was in order. These were the things I could control. I'd wake up at all hours of the night to clean or iron, just to calm my mind. It was exhausting and overwhelming, and my family thought I was losing it.

In 2019, I reached a breaking point. Fear had been my companion for so long that I didn't even know who I was without it. I was tired of feeling trapped, and as my walk with the Lord grew deeper, I knew it was time to surrender. The years of fear had taken a toll on my body—I struggled with insomnia, and the sleepless nights left me drained. It strained my marriage and my relationship with my kids, who I've since asked to forgive me.

It broke my heart to realize that I hadn't fully trusted God with my children. The truth is, He loves them even more than I do. For fifteen years, I had walked away from serving the Lord. I didn't have the personal relationship with Jesus that I have today. I tried to surrender many times, but real surrender didn't happen until I got on my knees and gave everything to God.

Someone once told me to write a letter to fear, and I had no idea how freeing that would be. As I began to write, the Lord gently revealed how much fear had ruled my heart. Fear had whispered lies, stolen my peace, and kept me from trusting Him. But as my words poured out, so did His truth—and in that moment, I felt the weight begin to lift.

I was reminded that fear has no authority where God's love dwells. Writing that letter felt like breaking chains I didn't even know I was carrying. "There is no fear in love; but perfect love casts out fear, because fear involves torment. But he who fears has not been made perfect in love" (1 John 4:18 NKJV).

Two main verses became my anchors during this season:

"Have I not commanded you? Be strong and of good courage; do not be afraid, nor be dismayed, for the Lord your God *is* with you wherever you go" (Joshua 1:9 NKJV).

And "I sought the Lord, and He heard me, and delivered me from all my fears" (Psalm 34:4 NKJV). That verse says *all* my fears, not *some*.

Even after returning to Jesus, surrendering control was still a process, but through the Lord's grace, mercy, and patience, I've learned to truly let go and trust Him. Today, I don't have sleepless nights over fear anymore. I am blessed to have a praying momma, a loving family, great friends, and spiritual sisters who remind me daily what it means to lay fear at His feet and walk in faith.
I still have moments when fear tries to creep in, but now, I take those thoughts captive and give them to the Lord immediately. The enemy knows my triggers, but Jesus is my protector. Reading God's

Word reassures me of His love for me and my family. I never want to live bound by fear again.

Today, I trust the Lord completely—with my life, my family, and our future. His promises are true, and His peace covers it all. Prayer has become my greatest weapon and my daily act of surrender. I believe a generational curse of fear has been broken.

If you're reading this and fear has had a grip on your life, please know you're not alone. I understand what it feels like to live guarded—to try to protect everyone and everything around you because you've been hurt before. But I also know what it feels like to finally breathe again, to release it all and trust God completely.

He is faithful. Whatever fear you're facing today, give it to Him. Let His perfect love cover every part of your heart. Freedom is possible. Peace is possible. And the same God who delivered me can deliver you, too.

About the Author

Laura Costantino is making her debut as a co-author in **When She Finally Let Go**. She is a devoted wife, loving mother, and proud Nana to three beautiful grandchildren. A cherished daughter and sister, Laura is known for her generous spirit and joy in serving both her family and community.

Her greatest passion is following Jesus and sharing His love while faithfully pursuing His will. Laura has the honor of hosting the **Daughters of the King – East Bay Chapter**, where she creates a warm, welcoming space for women to be uplifted, empowered, and strengthened through prayer and the Word of God.

Connect with Laura

FB: https://www.facebook.com/joebri2423

Publisher's Reflection

Fear is a powerful force—it can hold us captive, control our choices, and convince us that safety lies in control. But as this story so beautifully reveals, fear loses its grip when love steps in. Through tragedy, heartbreak, and years of living behind emotional walls, she discovered that surrender isn't weakness—it's the pathway to healing.

Her honesty allows readers to see the quiet war that often rages inside those who appear strong on the outside but are silently struggling within. For decades, fear shaped her thoughts and habits, but God, in His grace, patiently led her back to peace. The turning point came when she recognized that trust in God requires release—the willingness to let go of control and believe that His protection is greater than her precautions.

What stands out most is her courage to face what once terrified her and to speak the truth aloud: *fear has no authority where God's love dwells.* Her story is more than survival—it's transformation. It reminds us that even after years of pain, it's never too late to reclaim peace, rebuild faith, and break the chains that try to follow us into the next generation.

Through her surrender, she didn't just find freedom—she created a legacy of faith for her children and grandchildren. Her testimony is a powerful reminder that perfect love truly does cast out fear, and that trusting God with what we value most opens the door to lasting peace.

— *Dr. Paulette Harper*
Publisher & Visionary, *When She Finally Let Go*

The Words Within Her
Lisa Council

Words have power. They shape how we see ourselves, how we move through the world, and what we believe is possible. I learned this truth early.

As a little girl, I often heard the saying, "Sticks and stones may break your bones, but words will never hurt you." But my life tells a different story. Words hurt. They cut deep, embedding themselves into the most fragile places in my heart.

By age nine, I had already absorbed a lifetime of labels. Elders and classmates commented on everything—my dark chocolate skin, my long flowing hair, my looks, my worth.

"You're too dark to be pretty."

"You're dumb, just like your parents."

"You'll never amount to anything."

These were not just careless remarks; they became the soundtrack of my childhood.

I learned to keep my pain hidden. In my world, children were seen and not heard. So, I carried those words silently—words that told me I was unacceptable, unworthy, and unloved. Over time, they shaped how I saw myself. I did not view myself through God's eyes; I viewed myself through a broken lens.

"For he who touches you touches the apple of His eye" (Zechariah 2:8 NKJV).

As I grew older, the damage deepened. Low self-esteem led to self-destructive choices and unhealthy relationships. I daydreamed about a different life but convinced myself it wasn't for me. My cocoon of pain became a strange kind of comfort—it was what I knew.

Somewhere in the middle of that darkness, a still, small voice began tugging at my heart: "There's more for you." Sometimes, I ignored it. But it grew louder, like a gentle pull on my heartstrings.

By the time I turned twenty-five, I could no longer dismiss the tugging. I woke up that birthday morning determined to change something. I got dressed, looked in the mirror, and for a moment, thought I saw hope staring back. But almost immediately, the familiar chorus returned: *You're worthless. You're not smart. You'll never be enough.*

On the surface, I was functioning—active in church, praying for others, encouraging everyone around me. But inside, words that were never mine to carry still bound me. I knew God's Word, but I struggled to believe it for myself.

"I will say of the LORD, '*He is* my refuge and my fortress; My God, in Him I will trust'" (Psalms 91:2 NKJV). I could quote this scripture, yet my trust felt distant and unreal.

Then came a breaking point. One night, exhausted from the weight of it all, I cried out to God—not with polished prayers, but with raw, desperate honesty. "God, I can't keep living like this. Take these words. Take this pain. I surrender it all to you."

That moment didn't erase my past, but it marked the beginning of a new future. For the first time, I felt something loosen, a release I couldn't manufacture on my own. The lies that had echoed for decades began to lose their grip.

Before I could fully embrace healing, I had to release what no longer served me. God began showing me the areas in my life that still held me captive—the mindsets, the pain, and others' opinions. One by one, He invited me to let them go so that I could walk in freedom and truth.

Letting go of others' negative words became easy when I completely surrendered to God. But letting go did not happen all at once. It took time, prayer, and a lot of honesty. For years, I carried what people had said about me. Their words shaped how I saw myself. I believed what they said more than what God said. First, I had to pray and meditate to see myself as the Father sees me.

Others' Views of Me

Damaged and broken people spoke harmful words over me. It took time and God's grace for me to begin seeing myself through His lens. Convincing myself that I was whole wasn't enough; true healing required transformation from within.

I had to renew my mind, both the way I thought and how I perceived myself. This process began as I built an intimate relationship with God through prayer, studying His Word, and learning to be still in the discomfort of growth. Through writing positive affirmations and speaking them aloud, I started rebuilding my confidence. I learned to express my emotions honestly, allowing truth to become my foundation.

As I practiced connecting my words to my feelings, I became more effective in communicating not only with others but also with myself. Most importantly, therapy and surrounding myself with people who had experienced similar pain from verbal and emotional abuse reminded me that I was not alone.

(Romans 12:2 NKJV) says, "And do not be conformed to this world, but be transformed by the renewing of your mind, that you may prove what *is* that good and acceptable and perfect will of God." My healing came through the transformation of my thoughts and aligning my life with God's Word.

I had to release unhealthy relationships and friendships without explaining myself to anyone, and I didn't make exceptions for anyone. If it was unhealthy, I let it go. During times when I didn't stand firm in the boundaries I had set for myself, God removed people on my behalf. This often showed up through not receiving invitations to events and gatherings, unreturned phone calls, or people simply treating me differently.

As I began recognizing that God was working for my good, the removals became easier for me to accept. God's releasing made room for new, better, and more authentic friendships.

(Isaiah 43:19 NKJV) says, "Behold, I will do a new thing, Now it shall spring forth; Shall you not know it? I will even make a road in the wilderness *And rivers in the desert.*"

The metamorphosis of my life sometimes left me feeling trapped and alone, but I made peace with God's efforts so that I could spread my butterfly wings and fly free.

I spoke over myself, encouraging and reminding myself of who I am in God. (Psalm 139:14 NKJV) says, "I will praise You, for I am fearfully *and* wonderfully made; Marvelous are Your works, And *that* my soul knows very well."

As I continued trusting in God's Word, the belief that I am beautiful in His eyes and fearfully and wonderfully made rooted deeply within me.

Letting go wasn't easy, but it was necessary. Every release made room for something new—something God had been waiting to place in my hands all along. In surrendering what no longer served me, I discovered the beauty of what I was meant to gain.

I found peace in believing what God says about me. I gained confidence that is rooted in Him rather than through the lens of others and found the courage to boldly be myself, no longer running from my true identity. I could finally embrace who God called me to be. I no longer harbor feelings of being unqualified, unworthy, or ashamed, nor do I seek validation from others.

Writing this chapter forced me to dig deep into my painful past that I had hidden so long from not only others, but also from myself. It has allowed me the openness to express myself courageously so that I can flourish into all that God has created me to be. Sharing my testimony has been a humbling and rewarding experience that has helped me to grow, overcome, and prepare myself for my journey through life as well as the world around me. I am a three-time best-selling author, but my testimony shared in these pages came with courage and God's hands and whispers with every stroke of the keyboard.

Continuing to share my truth boldly and unapologetically is my journey to healing, wholeness, and freedom. And in the midst of all things, I will keep my eyes on the Lord, and I will succeed and give Him the glory.

To the sister still struggling with the echoes of negative words, be assured that you are God's girl. From the crown of your head to the soles of your feet, you are uniquely and wonderfully made by God in His image. You are beautiful, bright, intelligent, and deserving of all your heart's desires.

Look in the mirror and smile back at your reflection. May you walk boldly, courageously, and unapologetically in God's calling for your life. Take your rightful place in this world and declare and decree that you are God's creation!

You are so much more than others' negative words. You are God's unique masterpiece.

"For we are His workmanship, created in Christ Jesus for good works, which God prepared beforehand that we should walk in them" (Ephesians 2:10 NKJV). Walk humbly, steadfastly, and boldly in who God uniquely made you to be.

God, I thank you for making me in your image. I thank you for molding and shaping me into who you called me to be. Father, I pray that those struggling to see themselves the way you do will be delivered from the strongholds of low self-esteem, self-hatred, negative words, and the views of others, and may they walk boldly into a life free of bondage. In Jesus' name, Amen.

About the Author

Lisa Council is the founder and CEO of Self-Healing Ignites Flourishing Transformation (S.H.I.F.T.), Inc., and the creator and host of the *S.H.I.F.T. Monthly Podcast*, which airs internationally on social media platforms and iHeartRadio. She is also the founder, and CEO of I Am Lynda's Voice, LLC, and a passionate National Domestic Violence Advocate.

She is a best-selling author, national public speaker, and co-author in **When She Finally Let Go**, where she shares her story of healing, purpose, and transformation. Lisa has courageously overcome 33 years of domestic violence, low self-esteem, and tragedy. Her story was featured in the award-winning web series that received "Best Web

Series" at the 2017 DC Black Film Festival. Lisa's greatest passion is empowering women and young girls—assuring them that they, too, can live free from bondage, be healed from adversity, and see themselves as God sees them.

Connect with Lisa

Facebook: Lisa Renee

IG: @LisaC

Publisher's Reflection

In ***The Words Within Her***, Lisa invites us into a deeply personal journey—one that exposes the silent power of words and the lifelong echoes they can leave upon the soul. Through her story, we are reminded that healing often begins where pain once tried to silence us.

Lisa's transparency is both brave and liberating. She writes with the raw honesty of a woman who has faced the mirror, confronted her reflection, and chosen to see herself as God does—fearfully and wonderfully made. Her words testify to the truth that what others speak *over* us does not define who God designed us to *be*.

So many women carry wounds wrapped in words—labels spoken in ignorance or pain that still whisper lies in adulthood. Yet Lisa's story stands as a living declaration that when we surrender those words to God, He rewrites the narrative. What once broke us becomes the very foundation of our transformation.

Through faith, therapy, and grace, she learned that letting go is not about forgetting—it's about reclaiming identity. It's about trading the world's definitions for divine truth.

To every woman who still hears the echoes of "not enough," may this chapter remind you: God has already called you chosen, beloved, and His workmanship. Healing begins when you start believing it.

— *Dr. Paulette Harper*

Publisher & Visionary, *When She Finally Let Go*

Bag Lady
Dr. LeAnn Cerise Hendrick

Hey, Sis, have you ever felt like a bag lady? I'm not talking about one pushing a cart down the street filled with all her possessions, but one carrying around years of pain, expectations, and unspoken burdens. Well, I was that woman.

The bags I carried couldn't be seen. Mine were invisible—packed with heartache, disappointments, and silent struggles I didn't know how to put down. Each one represented a piece of my past, a weight I had learned to carry alone.

A bag lady carries far more than she was ever meant to bear. It's the weight of feeling like you can't ask for help, the heaviness of believing you're not worthy enough to share your struggles. It's the fear that if you do open up, someone might use your pain against you or manipulate your vulnerability.

As a young woman, I had already faced more than my share of turbulent times, so it was no surprise that I carried around some heavy bags. Some of them I tied with double knots because I didn't want the contents to spill out. Inside were the silent struggles of a victim of domestic violence, the grief of multiple divorces, toxic relationships, negative comments, the pain of losing pregnancies, the heartbreak of burying both of my parents—and the unbearable sorrow of losing my child. In one marriage, I was tormented and treated like trash because my abuser didn't respect me. A pastor told me to stop being weak, suck it up, and go home to be the submissive wife the Bible says to be.

It paralyzed me to the point that I wanted to give up on life. I struggled to make it but refused to ask anybody for help. After all, it was my stuff, and I was the only one who needed to see it. I didn't have anybody to tell me to put all those bags down.

The bags I carried hindered me in so many ways I didn't realize yet. I had been raised to figure it out on my own. Every struggle I fought to overcome and every loss I endured accumulated at an alarming rate, and I became a pro at tossing all these things into bags.

Those bags didn't just appear out of nowhere—they started long before adulthood. As a young girl, I had huge shoes to fill: maintaining good grades, joining the school chorus, serving as a crossing guard, participating in 4H and Glee Club, and dancing with my dance school. I was expected to excel at everything, and while I had plenty of dreams and goals, the pressure often left me overwhelmed. As I got older, that weight never lifted. The feeling of never being quite good enough followed me into adulthood and became one more bag I learned to carry. Sometimes, we don't realize that we become the living blooms of the seeds planted in us as children.

In fact, some of those issues carried over into motherhood. I began placing those same expectations and demands on my children. As a mom raising children alone, I pushed them to succeed because I never wanted people to say they were failures. I used to think that if I could do it this way, surely, they could, too. I pushed my children to the max and forced all of them to participate in activities.

It became so normal for me to carry these emotional bags from my past that I had no idea they were causing problems in my physical and spiritual life. I developed a caffeine addiction and used it as my coping mechanism, which led to insomnia, headaches when I couldn't get enough, and constant irritability.

All these bags I carried grew heavier. People began to notice—friends, relatives, even church members could see the pressure and strain. Several people told me to make myself a priority, to step back, rest, and pray before I drove myself crazy. I was only getting three hours of sleep a night. I isolated myself and, for a while, lost that social butterfly personality everyone knew me for. Depression settled in, and I wanted to throw in the towel.

I remember the turning point like it was yesterday. I was sitting in church one Sunday when the preacher's words pierced straight through me: "How long will you carry around the unnecessary weight? How long will you allow your past to hold you hostage? How long will you use the bags as an excuse to just barely make it by?"

I sat there in awe, frozen in my seat, wondering how he could be speaking directly to me when I hadn't told anybody what I was struggling with. It was as if God Himself had handed him my story. Could people tell I was carrying all that baggage? I was in shock, yet I felt relief. Even if no one else knew, Jesus surely did.

As the Lord ministered to me through that sermon, tears began to flow. I wept like a baby. I longed for relief, and for the first time, I embraced it. Something had to change, and help was available if I was willing to step forward.

As I sought the Lord for more clarity, He began speaking to me in dreams. He showed me what was lacking and what I needed to do to be delivered from the baggage. He told me to put the bags down—all at once. I'll admit, I was nervous and uncertain, but I knew God wouldn't leave me vulnerable without covering and protection. I knew this would be the healing I needed to be fully used by God. What I didn't anticipate was how liberating it would be.

I found myself desperate and ready to surrender what I thought was normal. I decided that I would put the bags down, step back, and never pick them up again. On that day, I let go of the shame, the guilt, the trauma, the embarrassment, the lies I had believed, the expectations others placed on me, and the ridicule that had kept me in bondage. That day, my life was renewed because I chose to put down all the bags and cry out to the Lord for help.

God immediately took the weights and shackles off me and began a new work in me, just as He promises in (Philippians 1:6 KJV): "Being confident of this very thing, that He which hath begun a good work in you will perform it until the day of Jesus Christ." I surrendered it all without regret. I said, "Lord, please take it all—I don't want it. You can have it."

The devil lost, and God prevailed in my life. I felt renewed in my mind, body, and soul. I was physically refreshed and ready to walk my new journey.

Putting down the bags made me a better mother to my children because it allowed me to extend grace and understand that they each have their own way of doing things. It made me a better employee because I had more clarity and energy. It made me a better friend and a friendlier neighbor because I was more in tune with life and saw things from a new perspective. Most importantly, it made me a better servant in the house of God. I felt as if I were living in heaven on earth. I slept peacefully at night, my headaches disappeared, I began eating again, and I started treating myself with care.

God did a great work within me after I let go of those bags. I was so excited about my new beginning that I immediately began sharing the good news with others. I told all the bag ladies—and the men, too—to let those bags go. I wanted women to know that it's not necessary for us to carry it all. Trying to bear every burden is not a requirement or the recipe for being a good woman, wife, or mother. I told the men they didn't have to be the trash man or live as prisoners in their past. I wanted everyone to drop those bags, leave them there, and never think about picking them up again. I felt an urgency to share this good news because I wanted others to be free to live a life full of love.

Christ already carried our baggage to the cross. He already suffered for our sake. If we are holding on to bags full of things that don't help us become better servants of the Lord, it's time to let them go. And if we must carry anything, let it be the things found in (Galatians 5:22–23 KJV): "But the fruit of the Spirit is love, joy, peace, longsuffering, gentleness, goodness, faith, meekness, temperance: against such there is no law."

Sis, I urge you to examine yourself today and see if you have some bags to unpack, put down, or toss out. What bags are you carrying that are stopping you from reaching your full potential in life, or from being a better servant? If you lack clarity, ask the Lord to expose your baggage and help you purge it as only He can. God provides us with a precise, complete, and clear understanding when we dwell in His presence.

"Let us lay aside every weight, and the sin which doth so easily beset us, and let us run with patience the race that is set before us" (Hebrews 12:1 KJV).

Allow God to lift your burdens so that you can be all that He has purposed and created you to be.

About the Author

Dr. LeAnn Cerise Hendrick is the founder and owner of Beyond The Call, Inc., Beyond The Call, LLC, and Sacred Praise Dance Ministry. She is a multiple best-selling author and contributing writer for the international best-selling *Listen Linda Magazine.* A prophetic liturgical dance minister, mobile notary, domestic violence advocate, motivational speaker, financial broker, and devoted servant of the Lord, Dr. Hendrick has dedicated more than 30 years to serving others with compassion and purpose.

Her faith-driven leadership and humanitarian work have earned her numerous honors, including a Honorary Doctorate in Christian Leadership, the Presidential Lifetime Achievement Award, the

Resilient Woman of the Year Award, the *Listen Linda Women of Excellence Award*, and the *Speak Up Sis Giver and Good Heart Award.*

She is also a featured co-author in the inspiring anthology **Women Who Finally Let Go**.

Connect with LeAnn

Website: www.beyondthecalling.com

Email: lhendrick@beyondthecalling.com

Publisher's Reflection

There are stories that move us, and then there are stories that *free us*. LeAnn's testimony does both.

In **Bag Lady**, she takes us by the hand and walks us through a journey so many women know too well—carrying invisible loads we were never created to bear. Pain tucked behind a smile. Expectations disguised as strength. Trauma masked as survival. Bags packed with years of silent battles, yet worn as if they were badges of honor.

Her honesty reminds us that healing doesn't always begin with knowing *what to do*—sometimes, it begins with admitting we've been carrying what we were never meant to hold.

What I love most about LeAnn's story is the moment she realized that surrender is not weakness—it is worship. When she let go, God stepped in. When she loosened her grip, deliverance met her right where she was. And in that surrender, she discovered a freedom she didn't even know existed—a lightness that only Jesus can bring.

Her transformation is a reminder that release is a spiritual act. Letting go is not losing—it is gaining room for God to breathe new life, new strength, and new identity into us.

Sis, as you read this chapter, I pray you take inventory of the bags in your own heart. Not to feel shame—but to feel *seen*. To feel invited into the same grace that met LeAnn. You don't have to carry it all. You don't have to figure it out alone. Sometimes, your greatest breakthrough is waiting on the other side of surrender.

Today, may you do what LeAnn courageously did: Put it down. Step back. And trust God to carry what you no longer can.

Because freedom is not just possible—it's promised.

— *Dr. Paulette Harper*
Publisher & Visionary, *When She Finally Let Go*

Shattered Pieces
Lisa Richmond

Have you ever carried words that were never meant to define you?

For years, I shouldered the burden of a toxic relationship—one steeped in betrayal, emotional abuse, and dishonesty. Each day, I struggled against an unseen force pulling me deeper into despair. My breaking point came during two pivotal moments. The first was when he sneered, "You'll never be as good as those other mothers. They actually know how to care for their children." That remark shattered my confidence, leaving me questioning my abilities as a mother. The second moment was a late-night argument when he coldly stated, "No one else will ever love you. You should be grateful I even stay." Those words echoed in my mind, eroding my self-worth and convincing me that I wasn't pretty enough, strong enough, or deserving of genuine love.

There were moments when his lies and deceit trapped me in a cage. He was the primary financial provider, and the thought of leaving felt impossible, especially while raising a child together. My decisions weighed on me; he scrutinized every move I made, and his expectations burdened my every thought. Trapped in this cycle, I often felt a physical heaviness in my chest, a constant reminder of my limitations and fears.

I fell into a deep depression. In search of solace, I turned to food to escape, using it to fill the void left by his hurtful words and my shattered self-esteem. Each binge provided temporary relief, a fleeting moment of comfort that quickly faded, leaving me feeling even more lost and unworthy. This cycle of emotional pain and unhealthy coping mechanisms only reinforced the belief that I was trapped in a life where love and acceptance hovered perpetually out of reach.

As his words sank deeper into my psyche, I began believing him. One evening, after yet another round of his harsh criticisms, I found myself sitting alone in my dimly lit living room, tears streaming down my face. His words wrapped around me like a heavy blanket, suffocating and inescapable. A profound sense of unworthiness enveloped me, stripping my identity.

Tightness gripped my chest, a physical manifestation of my despair. My heart raced, and my stomach churned with anxiety as I replayed his hurtful comments in my mind. I thought about how I had let my dreams slip away, convinced that I was not capable of achieving anything worthwhile. Rather than reaching out to family and friends for support, I isolated myself, believing that they would only see me as a failure. I avoided gatherings, opting instead to stay home, where I could hide from judgment and disappointment.

My choices were driven by the belief that I wasn't enough—enough as a mother, enough as a partner, and enough as a person. I stopped pursuing hobbies I once loved, convinced they were pointless endeavors. Instead, I sank into a routine of self-doubt and loneliness, fading into the background of my own life. This deep-seated belief in my unworthiness created a cycle of depression that felt inescapable, feeding into the isolation that reinforced my feelings of inadequacy.

What lies have you been holding onto that you need to release?

For me, trapped looked like endless days spent in a home filled with tension, where every conversation felt like a negotiation and anxiety laced every moment. It meant watching as he managed our finances, often masking the reality of our mounting debts while I struggled to make ends meet with the small allowance he provided for our child's needs. I would sit at the kitchen table, bills laid out before me, feeling the weight of responsibility resting solely on my shoulders, knowing I had no means to change our situation.

Yet, amid the darkness, a flicker of hope began to emerge. In 2011, a wake-up call altered the trajectory of my life. It was the moment I realized I had to take my power back. I confronted my past, making the difficult decision to sever ties with relationships that no longer contributed to my growth. I recognized the unhealthy beliefs I had internalized over the years: that I was unlovable, unworthy of success, and incapable of change. I had to let go of these beliefs and the patterns that had shaped my life—patterns of self-doubt, fear of rejection, and a tendency to prioritize others' needs above my own.

This realization, though painful, became a necessary step toward healing. I learned that true recovery required a profound emotional and spiritual surrender.

Emotionally, I began by feeling the full weight of my pain—no longer suppressing my emotions or pretending everything was okay. I would sit with my feelings, whether it was sadness, anger, or fear, acknowledging each one without judgment. Journaling became my outlet, where I poured out my thoughts and emotions, processing my experiences. I sought therapy, allowing a professional to guide me through my emotional turmoil and offer insights that I had been blind to.

Spiritually, I embarked on a journey of self-discovery. I explored mindfulness and meditation, which helped me connect with a deeper sense of self and find peace amid the chaos. I began letting go of the need to control every aspect of my life, learning to trust in the healing process. I sought practices that nourished my soul, such as spending time in nature, engaging in creative outlets, and surrounding myself with positive influences.

Through these practices, I gradually surrendered my old beliefs and patterns, opening myself up to new possibilities and a more authentic version of myself. This journey of emotional and spiritual surrender was transformative, empowering me to embrace vulnerability and cultivate resilience as I moved toward a brighter future.

I sought solace through prayer, reaching out to God for guidance and strength. These moments of stillness allowed me to connect with a deeper part of myself and find clarity. During this reflection, I made a solemn promise to myself and to God: I would never again permit anyone to inflict pain upon me. This commitment fueled my determination to focus on what truly mattered—my health, my children, and my education.

I enrolled in culinary school, immersing myself in my passion for cooking, which provided an outlet for creativity and self-expression. Later, I transitioned to City Vision University, where I earned an associate's degree.

Parts of my story may echo pieces of your own. You may be standing in a place where pain has spoken louder than truth, but that doesn't have to be the end. Healing is possible, and freedom is closer than you think. Take a moment to reflect on what you've been carrying and give yourself permission to release it. Your next chapter begins the moment you believe that you're worthy of more.

About the Author

Lisa Richmond is a Certified Life Coach, Recovery Coach, and ordained minister based in Lake County, Illinois. A bestselling author featured in *The 2nd Wind Anthology*, she is a passionate advocate for mental health awareness and emotional resilience. Drawing from her personal experiences with trauma, addiction, and grief, Lisa empowers others to embrace healing, restoration, and renewed purpose.

In addition to her coaching and writing, Lisa is a dynamic speaker who shares powerful insights at conferences and workshops, inspiring audiences to overcome adversity and live authentically. She believes in the transformative power of storytelling and encourages others to use their voices as instruments of healing and hope.

Lisa is also a co-author in *When She Finally Let Go*, her second collaborative book, where she shares a heartfelt message of faith, perseverance, and the freedom found through surrender.

Connect with Lisa

Email: meidentity336@gmail.com

Website: https://www.lisa-richmond.com

Publisher's Reflection

Lisa's story is a powerful reminder of how words—especially those spoken in moments of cruelty—can shape the way we see ourselves. For years, she carried the weight of lies meant to diminish her, not realizing that those words were never hers to own. Her journey reflects what so many women silently endure: living beneath labels that God never placed on them. Yet what moves me most is the moment she decided to take her power back, to release the lies, and to rewrite her narrative with truth, faith, and resilience.

Sis, maybe you've also carried words that were never meant to define you. Perhaps pain has spoken louder than purpose, or fear has whispered lies about your worth. Lisa's story is proof that healing begins the moment we confront those lies and surrender them to God. Letting go is not denial—it's divine alignment. It's the courageous act of releasing what broke you so you can embrace what's waiting to build you.

When Lisa chose to let go, she didn't just reclaim her voice—she stepped into her next chapter with determination, faith, and purpose. Her story reminds us that even in our most shattered seasons, God is able to take the broken pieces and create something beautiful. He doesn't waste pain; He transforms it.

Take a moment and ask yourself: What words have you allowed to shape your identity that God never spoke? What weight are you still carrying that it's time to release? Healing begins with that decision. Your story, like Lisa's, is still being written—and the next chapter can be one of restoration, strength, and freedom.

— *Dr. Paulette Harper*
Publisher & Visionary, *When She Finally Let Go*

Calling All Readers!

Have you been moved, inspired, or set free by **When She Finally Let Go**? We'd love to hear how these powerful stories have impacted your heart and strengthened your faith.

Your voice matters—your reflection could be the spark that helps another woman find healing, courage, and hope.

Here's how you can make a difference:

- Visit the book's page on your favorite online retailer.

- Leave a heartfelt review sharing how *When She Finally Let Go* spoke to your journey.

- Encourage your sisters, friends, and community to read the book and experience **real stories, real breakthrough, real change.**

Every review you write helps spread a message of freedom and faith—reminding women everywhere that there is beauty in surrender and power in letting go.

Thank you for being part of this movement of women who choose healing, purpose, and divine transformation. Your support means everything!

Visionary Author Dr. Paulette Harper
www.pauletteharper.com

Thank you so much!!

Write a Book With Me

Do you have a story you want to share?

Would you like to be in our next anthology?

WHAT'S IN IT FOR YOU?

Instant credibility for writing a best-selling book

Your personal worth will increase

Speaking opportunities will open for you

Your personal finance will increase

Your personal brand will be connected with other like-minded people

Notoriety – Your circle of influence will increase and be empowered

JOIN ME!

I want to personally invite you to partner with me and join the waitlist for the next

anthology offered by Visionary Author Dr. Paulette Harper

Visit https://pauletteharper.com/opportunities/ to get on the waitlist for the next book collaboration.

Author Coaching Services

Offered by Dr. Paulette Harper

Join us at One Story University Online School.

Unlock The Writer In You 90 Day Program

One Story University is an online school that provides aspiring authors with a step-by-step process on how to write and publish their self-help, how to, and personal story books in 90 days.

Visit Unlock the Writer to get access to the course.

A group coaching program for coaches, speakers, thought leaders, and entrepreneurs who are ready to write, self- publish and launch a best- selling book in 90 days.

5 Module Outline

Module 1 **The Story Framework**-The purpose behind your book, getting clarity on your story and creating the outline is the foundation every writer needs in order to produce a great book. The best writers are those who can frame the outline of their content, ensuring each chapter flows consistently and concisely for the reader.

Module 2- **Crafting Your Story**- Writers must know their ideal audience so they craft content that compels, sells, and propels their readers. Creating a premise and promise statement assures you will achieve all three.

Module 3- **Constructing Your Book**- Putting your book all together requires knowing what goes in the front and back of your book, as well as, hiring the right literary team to help put your book together.

Module 4- **The Publishing Lab**- Now you're ready to learn the steps to finally publishing your book and securing your intellectual property.

Module 5 – **Promoting Your Book**- Before you can promote yourself and your book, you must establish a customized and focused marketing plan. Bringing a new book to the market will require a strategy, a vision and proper planning in order to generate book sales.

Visit Unlock the Writer to get access to the course. https://www.onestoryuniversity.com/unlock-the-writer

Other Books By
Dr. Paulette Harper

Do your need a Executive Book Mentor?
Visit https://pauletteharper.com/services/

Solo Books

Fiction Inspirational
Secret Places Revealed (Award winner)
Living Separate Lives

Children

Princess Neveah: Lessons of Self Discovery

Nonfiction

That Was Then, This Is Now: This Broken Vessel Restored
Completely Whole
Faith For Every Mountain
Coloring Book
The Scriptures in Color

Anthologies (Nonfiction)

The Breaking Point
When Queens Rise
For Such a Time as This
I Survived The Storm
Resilience in Hard Times
Women who Soar
Arise From The Ashes
Breaking The Silence
Her Unbreakable Spirit
Women with Unshakable Faith

Find my entire library of books on Amazon: https://www.amazon.com/stores/author/B004FEJKCQ

www.ingramcontent.com/pod-product-compliance
Lightning Source LLC
Chambersburg PA
CBHW071221160426
43196CB00012B/2375